Why Jesus?

John Blanchard

EP Books (Evangelical Press), 1st Floor Venture House, 6 Silver Court, Watchmead, Welwyn Garden City, UK, AL7 1TS

sales@epbooks.org   www.epbooks.org

In the USA EP Books are distributed by JPL Books, 3741 Linden Ave. S.E., Wyoming, MI 49548

Office:877-683-6935

order@jplbooks.com   www.jplbooks.com

First published 2016

British Library Cataloguing in Publication Data available
Print ISBN 978-1-78397-168-8
ePub ISBN 978-1-78397-169-5
Kindle ISBN 978-1-78397-170-1

Contents

Introduction

Religion has had a long shelf life, and in one form or another is here to stay. This is because as human beings we instinctively want to believe that our lives are not completely futile, and that we are part of something bigger, something that can give us purpose and value.

Yet anyone who wants to find the right religion is faced with a bewildering array of choices: Islam gets most of today's headlines, Hinduism and Buddhism draw millions, and Christianity is still growing. Most religions have a focus on a personality: Muslims acknowledge various leaders though no-one approaches the status of Mohammed; the Buddha's teaching is the foundation of the movement that takes his title and Christianity's fundamental focus is on a first-century Jew (Jesus) who died a criminal's death. Christianity claims that only through this man can our deepest religious needs be met, and that only through him can we get right with God.

Why Jesus?

This book will answer that question ...

1 Back to the Future

At first glance, the answer to the question at the end of the introduction seems far from obvious. One philosopher wrote, 'Historically, it is quite doubtful whether Jesus ever existed at all, and if he did we do not know anything about him,' but as he was an atheist he had a vested interest in writing that. Not surprisingly, the well-known atheist Richard Dawkins took more or less the same line and went no further than to say that 'Jesus probably existed.'

Turning from guesswork to certainties, nineteen celebrated authors in the first and second centuries, with no religious axes to grind, recorded more than 100 facts about Jesus, giving details of his birth, life, teaching and death, all without the slightest hint that he was not a real historical person. These writers included the Jewish historian Flavius Josephus; Suetonius, the official historian of the Roman imperial house; Cornelius Tacitus, another eminent historian who was also Governor of Asia; and Pliny the Younger, a Roman proconsul in Bithynia in Asia Minor and prolific letter writer. Their confirmation that Jesus was a real person and not a religious myth is all the more remarkable as they all rejected the main thrust of his teaching. As someone has said, the argument that Jesus never existed has been 'demolished' ... by 'the march of historical research'.

Almost all the data we have about Jesus is in the Bible and this will be our database from now on. The Old Testament records events before Jesus was born, and the New Testament takes over just before his birth. He was born about 2,000 years ago into a working-class Jewish family living in Nazareth, Israel. This meant that he started his earthly life on the wrong side of the tracks, not just because it was a small community in the backwoods of what was then part of the Roman Empire, but because of its very bad social reputation. It was so despised that somebody of Jesus' day asked a friend, 'Can anything good come out of Nazareth?' (John 1:46). In those days Nazareth (more a village than a town) was a small agricultural settlement with no trade routes, and so of no economic importance. It is not even mentioned in the Old Testament, which covers many centuries of Israel's history, so we can assume that nobody of national significance had any links with it.

Jesus was not actually born in Nazareth, but in Bethlehem, about seventy miles to the south, while his parents were there for a Roman census to be taken. When they got there, the town was so crowded that there was no normal accommodation available, and they had to make do with some kind of outhouse or stable. It was in these primitive surroundings that Jesus was born, the family returning to Nazareth soon afterwards. About two years later they emigrated to Egypt to escape a massacre of all male children in the neighbourhood under two years of age which was ordered by the ruthless (perhaps paranoid) King Herod, a puppet of the Roman Empire. After Herod died in Jericho in 4BC, Jesus' family returned to Nazareth and settled down there. From then on, other than an incident at a Jewish festival in Jerusalem when Jesus was twelve years old, the trail goes cold for about eighteen years; there is no record of anything he said or did during that time. Suddenly, everything changed...

The bombshell

The day the tide turned began quite normally when, as a devout Jew, Jesus attended a Sabbath day worship service in his local synagogue. During a typical service a passage of the Old Testament would be read, and on this occasion Jesus was invited to read it. When an attendant handed him a scroll containing part of the book of Isaiah he read these words:

> *The Spirit of the Lord is upon me, because he has anointed me to proclaim good news to the poor. He has sent me to proclaim liberty to the captives and recovering of sight to the blind, to set at liberty those who are oppressed, to proclaim the year of the Lord's favour.* (Luke 4:18-19)

So far so good; the Jews saw the Old Testament as not just a record of their nation's history, but God's word to them as his chosen people, and through them to the rest of humankind. Central to all of this was the promise that one day God would break into history by sending a great Jewish king who would meet man's deepest need and establish the kingdom of God. In the Old Testament one prophet after another spoke of a coming Messiah ('anointed one'), and the last of them, Malachi, repeated God's promise by writing that *the Lord whom you seek will suddenly come* (Malachi 3:1).

The words Jesus read from the scroll prophesied what the coming Messiah would say about himself, and the worshippers in the synagogue would have been familiar with them. When Jesus finished reading, it might have been expected that one of the leaders of the service would make some comments on it—perhaps assuring his listeners that although 400 years had passed since the last Old Testament prophecy, God remained true to his promise and Messiah would come. However, when he had finished reading Jesus sat down. Doing this would mean nothing to us today, but in the context of synagogue worship at that time it was a signal that he intended to say something else. This explains why suddenly *the eyes of all in the synagogue were fixed on him* (Luke 4:20).

Then came the bombshell ... Instead of the kind of pious platitudes his hearers may have heard many times before, Jesus announced, *Today this Scripture has been fulfilled in your hearing* (Luke 4:21). Nobody could possibly miss the point: Jesus was claiming that when Isaiah wrote about the coming Messiah he was referring to him. As he developed his claim and pressed home some of its implications his listeners were outraged, and eventually became so furious that they bundled him out of the synagogue and tried to throw him over a cliff. Somehow he escaped, and as far as we know he never returned to Nazareth.

This incident launched his public career, and we next read of him teaching in a synagogue in Capernaum, a fishing village on the Sea of Galilee, about forty miles to the north-east of Nazareth. Here, too, people were *astonished at his teaching* and recognized that *his word possessed authority* (Luke 4:32). From then on, his claim to be the Messiah promised by God became a fundamental feature of his teaching, and in pressing it home he drew on all three sections of the Old Testament—the law, the poetical books and the prophets.

Though there were times when the Jews side-stepped some of the things he had written, they looked on a man called Moses as God's great lawgiver, and Jesus told them point-blank, *If you believed Moses, you would believe me, for he wrote of me* (John 5:46).

The Psalms are the best known of the poetical books and contain many references to Messiah, and Jesus had no hesitation in claiming that these were all about him. For example, when he was being persecuted he said that this was in fulfilment of a psalm in which Messiah says, *They hated me without a cause* (John 15:25). Daniel, one of the prophets, foresaw the great deliverer as *one like a son of man* (Daniel 7:13)—and Jesus applied the title 'Son of Man' to himself seventy-eight times.

Jesus could not have been more consistent in his claims to be God's promised Messiah. Speaking to a group of religious leaders one day, he commended them for their study of the Old Testament and then condemned them for failing to see its meaning: *You search the Scriptures because you think that in them you have eternal life; and it is they that bear witness about me, yet you refuse to come to me that you may have life* (John 5:39-40). His message was crystal clear—but was it correct? In trying to find an answer to the question 'Why Jesus?' we dare not miss the significance of what the Bible's prophets wrote hundreds of years before he was born.

Advance announcements

We can begin with Abraham, who lived about 2,000 years before Jesus was born and was called by God to leave his hometown of Ur (in what may now be southern Iraq) to lead his family to a new country. The whole project was an exercise in faith, but in the course of calling him, God promised Abraham that *in you all the families of the earth shall be blessed* (Genesis 12:3). Nearly fifty years later God confirmed this by telling Abraham that *in your offspring shall all the nations of the earth be blessed* (Genesis 22:18). In the New Testament the genealogy of Jesus begins with Abraham (Matthew 1:2), confirming the first indication in Genesis that Messiah would come through Abraham's descendants. This means that 2,000 years before Jesus was born every family on earth except Abraham's was out of the running.

As we trace Abraham's family tree in the Bible, alongside references to a coming deliverer we see God overruling convention time and again, and renewing his promise through descendants not normally expected to inherit their parents' role. To squeeze hundreds of years into a sentence, Messiah would come from a line beginning with Abraham then running specifically through descendants called Jacob, Judah, Jesse and David—which precludes most of the human race. But we can add two further pointers. One of the prophecies said that Judah would continue providing Israel with its kings until Messiah came. Judah's government collapsed with the destruction of Jerusalem in AD70—and

Jesus was born just before the deadline expired; the prophecy's timing was perfect.

The second pointer is the Old Testament's prophecy of the town where Jesus would be born: *But you, O Bethlehem Ephrathah, who are too little to be among the clans of Judah, from you shall come forth for me one who is to be ruler in Israel* (Micah 5:2). There were two Bethlehems in the country, one in the region of Ephrathah in Judea and the other in Zebulon, seventy miles to the north. The prophecy is precise: Messiah would be born in the first of these and the New Testament tells us that *Jesus was born in Bethlehem of Judea* (Matthew 2:1).

Although these prophecies point strongly to Jesus, they are not enough to prove that he was Messiah—but there are nearly 300 others that put it beyond doubt. To begin with, there are prophecies about his position or 'office'. The Old Testament said that Messiah would be a prophet: *I will raise up for them a prophet ... he shall speak to them all that I command him* (Deuteronomy 18:18); and in the New Testament people said of Jesus, *A great prophet has arisen among us* (Luke 7:16). The Old Testament said that Messiah would be *a priest forever* (Psalm 110:4); and in the New Testament the quotation is applied word for word to Jesus (see Hebrews 5:6). The Old Testament said that Messiah would be a king: *I have set my king on Zion, my holy hill* (Psalm 2:6); and in the New Testament, Jesus told the Roman governor Pontius Pilate, *You say that I am a king. For this purpose I was born and for this purpose I have come into the world* (John 18:37). The Old Testament also sees Messiah as God's servant: *Behold my servant, whom I uphold, my chosen, in whom my soul delights* (Isaiah 42:1); and the New

Testament applies these words directly to Jesus (see e.g. Matthew 12:18).

That is not all; there are also many prophecies about the amazing things Messiah would do. Here is an excerpt from one of the most comprehensive:

> *Then the eyes of the blind shall be opened, and the ears of the deaf unstopped; then shall the lame man leap like a deer, and the tongue of the mute shout for joy* (Isaiah 35:5-6).

The New Testament specifically records Jesus as healing the blind, the deaf, the lame and the dumb. At one point, as a kind of interim summary, one writer reports that *Jesus went throughout all the cities and villages, teaching in their synagogues and proclaiming the gospel of the kingdom and healing every disease and every affliction* (Matthew 9:35). In ending his report, another goes even further and says, *Now there are also many other things that Jesus did. Were every one of them to be written, I suppose that the world itself could not contain the books that would be written* (John 21:25). I once heard someone suggest that Jesus simply read Old Testament prophecies, then set out to fulfil them so as to pass himself off as Messiah, but this is a ridiculous suggestion. Could anyone with inflated ideas of his own importance simply decide to go out and do all these things, especially when we remember that on three separate occasions Jesus raised people from the dead? (see e.g. Mark 5:21-43).

Death notices

But we have not yet touched on the amazingly accurate prophecies about the suffering Messiah would endure and the way in which he would meet his death. We might not expect prophecies about an all-conquering deliverer to concentrate on such things—but they do. Jesus was executed after being wrongly sentenced at a series of show trials on a string of false charges. In a later chapter we will look in detail at the importance of his death, but must not miss the fact that no fewer than twenty-nine prophecies, made centuries earlier, were fulfilled by Jesus in his final twenty-four hours on earth. Here are some of those predictions and their fulfilment.

• He would be forsaken by his followers: *Strike the shepherd, and the sheep will be scattered* (Zechariah 13:7). When Jesus was arrested, his closest followers *all left him and fled* (Mark 14:50).

• He would be wrongly accused: *Malicious witnesses rise up …* (Psalm 35:11). When Jesus was on trial, *Many false witnesses came forward* (Matthew 26:60).

• He would be ill-treated: *I gave my back to those who strike, and my cheeks to those who pull out the beard; I hid not my face from disgrace and spitting* (Isaiah 50:6). The New Testament records that at one point, *They spit in his face and struck him. And some slapped him, saying, "Prophesy to us, you Christ! Who is it that struck you?"* (Matthew 26:67-68).

• He would not retaliate: *He was oppressed, and he was afflicted, yet he opened not his mouth* (Isaiah 53:7). When being bullied by Pilate, Jesus *gave him no answer, not even to a single charge* (Matthew 27:14).

• He would be executed with criminals: *He poured out his soul to death and was numbered with the transgressors* (Isaiah 53:12). When Jesus was executed, *Two robbers were crucified with him, one on the right and one on the left* (Matthew 27:38).

• He would be put to death by crucifixion: *They have pierced my hands and feet* (Psalm 22:16). The New Testament records that *When they came to the place that is called The Skull, there they crucified him* (Luke 23:33). (What makes this one of the most remarkable fulfilments of prophecy is that David, who wrote that Psalm, was a Jew and the Jews never practised crucifixion; it was not until centuries later that the Romans did so—and initially only as a form of punishment, not for carrying out a death sentence).

• He would pray for his executioners: *He ... makes intercession for the transgressors* (Isaiah 53:12). While hanging on the cross, Jesus prayed, *Father, forgive them, for they know not what they do* (Luke 23:34).

• None of his bones would be broken: *The Lord ... keeps all his bones, not one of them is broken* (Psalm 34:19-20). On the day Jesus was executed soldiers broke the legs of the two criminals to ensure their death and the removal of the bodies before the Sabbath, *But when they came to Jesus and saw that he was already dead, they did not break his legs* (John 19:33).

• His body would be pierced: *They look on me, on him whom they have pierced* (Zechariah 12:10). The New Testament records that to confirm his death, instead of breaking his legs, *one of the soldiers pierced his side with a spear ...* (John 19:34).

• People would gamble for his clothing: *They divide my garments among them, and for my clothing they cast lots* (Psalm 22:18). John says, *When the soldiers had crucified Jesus, they took his garments and divided them into four parts, one part for each soldier; also his tunic. But the tunic was seamless, woven in one piece from top to bottom, so they said to one another, "Let us not tear it, but cast lots for it to see whose it shall be"* (John 19:23-24).

These are just a few examples of over 300 prophecies fulfilled to the letter in the life and death of this one man. Any talk of Jesus having 'fixed' these things to bolster his claim to be God's Messiah can safely be ignored. But did they all coincide by chance? This idea becomes absurd when we bring mathematics to bear on the case.

Some years ago a newspaper carried the story of a married couple who had just won an overseas holiday in a raffle held at a travel fair. As there were 799 other tickets in the draw, the odds against them doing so were 800 to one. There was nothing newsworthy about that, but the story got the media's attention because the couple had then won the same raffle three years running and the odds against that were calculated at 50,000,000 to one. Those odds are breath-taking—yet they are tiny compared to the odds against Jesus fulfilling the Old Testament's Messianic prophecies by chance.

Why Jesus? Because nobody else in human history had hundreds of prophecies about his birth, character, life and death made hundreds of years before he was born—all of which were fulfilled to the letter.

2 Family News

One person's entry into the world is very much like another's: conception, pregnancy, labour, delivery—and unless there are unusual complications or other significant factors biographers spend little or no time on these. But when we begin to examine the record of Jesus' life there is no way in which we can treat his arrival into the world as ordinary. Before we see why, we can begin by noting a couple of uncertainties.

Although Jesus' birth is celebrated globally on 25 December every year (smothered with many things that have nothing whatsoever to do with his birth) it is virtually certain that it was not on that date. One clue is that on the day he was born in Bethlehem *there were shepherds out in the field, keeping watch over their flocks by night* (Luke 2:8). By the end of December the temperature in Bethlehem would have dropped to something near zero, and sheep would by then have been brought in from the fields for shelter during the winter. We are also unsure of the exact year when Jesus was born. We know it was *in the days of Herod the king* (Matthew 2:1), which still gives a time slot of over forty years. However, as we saw in the previous chapter, Jesus' family returned to Nazareth from exile in Egypt immediately after Herod died in 4 BC, and Jesus was still a *child* (Matthew 2:21) at that time. With no other data to go on, we have to accept that any suggested dates for his birth year are no more than well-meaning guesses.

So much for the uncertainties; now we come to the facts, and to the one that marks Jesus out from the rest of the entire human race: when Jesus was born his mother was a virgin. This is usually referred to as the 'virgin birth', but that is rather misleading, as nothing unusual is recorded about his birth. What is unique is not how he left his mother's womb, but how he entered it, and on this the Bible is clear. There is no small print, and no 'ifs' or 'buts'. It says that Jesus was conceived in his mother's womb without sexual intercourse, and without any rupture of the hymen. In medical terms, his mother became pregnant while still *virgo intacta*. Nor is there any mileage in pointing out that *in vitro* fertilization, embryonic transfer or artificial insemination now make it perfectly possible for a woman to give birth without direct sexual intercourse, as in all of these cases male sperm is needed—and in the case of Jesus there was none.

The matter of miracles

Some readers may be tempted to switch off at this point, and say that the idea of a woman giving birth without receiving male sperm in one way or another is either complete nonsense or suggests a miracle—and miracles are nothing more than religious mumbo-jumbo. The point is so important that we need to look at it very closely—and begin by defining what a miracle is.

Simply put, a miracle is something that contradicts the scientific laws governing our present world of time and space, and for some people that clinches things; they say that miracles cannot and do not happen. In a letter to *The Times* when the question of miracles was hitting the headlines, thirteen prominent scientists, most of them university professors, made the point well: 'It is not logically valid to use science as an argument against miracles. To believe that miracles cannot happen is as much an act of faith as to believe that they can happen ... miracles are unprecedented events. Whatever the current fashions in philosophy or the revelations of opinion polls may suggest, it is important to affirm that science ... can have nothing to say on the subject.'

When considering the possibility of an alleged miracle having taken place, the only sensible approach is to look at the available data with an open mind, assess its value, then come to an honest conclusion as to where the evidence points. In the case of the virgin conception of Jesus, the problem is not the reliability of the evidence, but the prejudice that people bring to the case. Ultimately the question is not 'Can miracles happen?' but 'Have they happened?', and the right way to find the answer is to set aside personal opinions and prejudices and examine each event in the light of the evidence.

Ante-natal reports

On the birth of Jesus, it is interesting to note that the only direct records we have come from the pens of two New Testament writers, Matthew and Luke, both men whose occupations called for accuracy and attention to detail. Matthew was a civil servant working in Capernaum as a tax collector for the occupying Romans. An intelligent man, who understood both Hebrew and Greek, he would have needed to be careful about keeping accurate records. Luke was a medical doctor, and his writing illustrates his meticulous attention to detail. While another New Testament writer tells us about a man with *a withered hand* (Mark 3:1), Luke says that the man's *right hand was withered* (Luke 6:6). While Matthew says that someone's mother-in-law had *a fever* (Matthew 8:14), Luke says she was *ill with a high fever* (Luke 4:38), using exactly the right medical word to identify the serious condition. This kind of attention to detail suggests that he would hardly invent a story which would contradict all his medical knowledge and make him the laughing-stock of his fellow physicians. Bearing these two facts in mind, we can turn to look at their testimonies. Matthew's report runs like this:

> *Now the birth of Jesus Christ took place in this way. When his mother had been betrothed to Joseph, before they came together she was found to be with child from the Holy Spirit. And her husband Joseph, being a just man and unwilling to put her to shame, resolved to divorce her quietly. But as he considered these things, behold, an angel of the Lord appeared to him in a dream, saying, 'Joseph, son of David, do not fear to take Mary as your wife, for that which is*

conceived in her is from the Holy Spirit. She will
bear a son, and you shall call his name Jesus, for he
will save his people from their sins' (Matthew
1:18-21).

He then adds, *When Joseph woke from sleep, he did as the
angel of the Lord commanded him: he took his wife, but knew
her not until she had given birth to a son. And he called his name
Jesus* (Matthew 1:24-25).

Matthew begins by telling us that Mary was 'betrothed'
to Joseph. The first stage in a traditional Jewish marriage was
engagement, an informal arrangement that was sometimes
made by the parents of the couple concerned. The second
was betrothal, when the couple pledged themselves to each
other before witnesses. They would then be considered
husband and wife, though they would not live together.
About a year later, they moved to formal marriage, when
they would set up home together. This explains why
Matthew refers to Joseph as Mary's 'husband' and the angel
calls Mary Joseph's 'wife', even though at that stage they were
only betrothed.

Joseph was shattered by the news of Mary's pregnancy. As
he was not the father, he could only think that Mary had
cheated on him—and as far as he was concerned the
marriage was off. Betrothal was such a serious step that
ending it would need a divorce, which could be secured in
one of two ways. The first would mean a court case, when
Mary would have to confess to her adultery, leaving her
reputation in shreds; from then on she would be treated as
damaged goods. The only other option (abortion was never
on the agenda) would mean handing her what was known as
a bill of divorcement in the presence of two witnesses.

Straightforward justice called for a court case, but because of his love for Mary and his concern for her welfare Joseph decided on the second option: he *resolved to divorce her quietly* (Matthew 1:19).

However, while he was thinking about this, God told him to go ahead with the marriage, because Mary's pregnancy was not the result of adultery but of God's miraculous intervention. God also told Joseph that the child would be a boy and was to be called Jesus. This was a common name at the time, but the final part of God's message explained why it was to be given. The word 'Jesus' means 'Saviour' and Jesus was to have the name *for he will save his people from their sins*. This must have been way over Joseph's head, but he did as he was told and the marriage went ahead. Now legally married, Joseph and Mary were free to have a normal physical relationship, but Matthew specifically adds that Joseph 'knew her not until she had given birth to a son'. This makes it clear that when Jesus was born Mary was still a virgin.

As we might expect of a doctor, Luke's version of events focuses on Mary:

> *In the sixth month the angel Gabriel was sent from God to a city of Galilee named Nazareth, to a virgin betrothed to a man whose name was Joseph, of the house of David. And the virgin's name was Mary. And he came to her and said, 'Greetings, O favoured one, the Lord is with you!' But she was greatly troubled at the saying and tried to discern what sort of greeting this might be. And the angel said to her, 'Do not be afraid, Mary, for you have found favour with God. And behold, you will conceive in your womb and bear a son, and you shall call his name*

> *Jesus. He will be great and will be called the Son of the Most High. And the Lord God will give to him the throne of his father David, and he will reign over the house of Jacob for ever, and of his kingdom there will be no end.' And Mary said to the angel, 'How will this be, since I am a virgin?' And the angel answered her, 'The Holy Spirit will come upon you, and the power of the Most High will overshadow you; therefore the child to be born will be called holy —the Son of God'* (Luke 1:26-35).

As Mary was not yet pregnant, this incident obviously took place before the one recorded by Matthew. For an angel to appear and tell her that in some special way she had found favour with God was amazing enough, but what followed stunned her: she was to give birth to a son and (just as the angel had told Joseph) she must call him Jesus. Her immediate response was understandable: *How will this be, since I am a virgin?* Mary knew that to give birth she would need to conceive, and as she had never slept with Joseph or with any other man, and had no intention of having sexual intercourse with Joseph before her marriage to him, how could she become pregnant?

The angel's reply was the same as the one soon to be given to Joseph. God would cause a biological miracle to take place in her womb and she would conceive while remaining a virgin. As a result, she would give birth to a boy, who would not be the son of Joseph, but uniquely the Son of God.

Mary was totally baffled, but the angel reminded her of a miracle that had recently taken place within her own family: *And behold, your relative Elizabeth in her old age has also conceived a son, and this is the sixth month with her who was called barren. For nothing will be impossible with God* Luke 1:36-37). As Mary knew that Elizabeth was well past child-bearing age, the angel's news convinced her that God truly was at work in her own situation and she replied, *Behold, I am the servant of the Lord; let it be to me according to your word* (Luke 1:38).

Luke's ante-natal report ends there, and its special interest to us is that three times it states that Mary was a virgin when she conceived Jesus in her womb. When recording the beginning of Jesus' public ministry thirty years later, Luke called him *the son (as was supposed) of Joseph* (Luke 3:23). This tells us that people assumed Jesus was Joseph's son; Luke knew otherwise.

Alternatives?

The testimonies of Matthew and Luke are clear, but sceptics are reluctant to believe them, and have come up with a number of other theories aimed at explaining what may have happened. We can mention some of them here.

Early sceptics said that virgin conception was a myth created to cover up the fact that Jesus was fathered by a Roman soldier named Panthera or Pandira, but this is clutching at non-existent straws, as there is not a shred of evidence to back it up.

Some say that the 'virgin birth' of Jesus was invented by his followers to outdo stories about pagan gods. For example, Buddha's mother claimed that a white elephant with six tusks 'entered my belly'. The mother of the Greek god Perseus was supposed to have been impregnated by a shower of golden rain containing the supreme god Zeus, who had quite a reputation for impregnating women in bizarre ways. He was even said to have turned himself into a serpent to fertilize Olympias, the wife of the Macedonian monarch Philip of Macedon, an escapade that led to the birth of Alexander the Great. These grotesque stories bear no resemblance to the Bible's record of the virgin conception, which has no pagan parallel. Can we really imagine a respectable Jew like Matthew, committed to the highest moral standards, inventing something that would outdo the most outrageous and bizarre birth-myths in pagan culture, then declaring this to be God's work?

Others suggest that because the Jews were rather puritanical about sexual matters and considered sexual intercourse to be 'unclean' they invented a story that shied away from any suggestion that Jesus came about as the result of a physical relationship between a husband and wife. This idea is ridiculous, as the Bible has a robustly healthy attitude towards sex within the bounds of marriage.

Another approach is to suggest that the virgin conception of Jesus was a case of parthenogenesis, a form of reproduction in which embryos or seeds grow and develop in the female of the species without fertilization by a male. This is extremely unusual, though it does occur in a few plants (such as roses and orange trees), and in certain fish, amphibians, birds, and reptiles. It has also been noted in sharks, whiptails, geckos, rock lizards and some other creatures—but never naturally in mammals.

In any case, this cannot have happened in the case of Jesus, for one very simple reason. In the genetic make-up of human beings, the male has x and y chromosomes, while the female has x and x. If Mary's pregnancy had been triggered by some unique biological freak, the baby would have been female, as there would have been no y chromosome present to produce a male.

All of these feeble attempts to discredit the only contemporary evidence we have ignore one simple fact. As God brought all the laws of nature into existence, surely he has the right to suspend any of them to fulfil his own purposes? However unlikely they may appear to us, miracles are not a problem to God, for whom there is no distinction between the natural and the supernatural. Natural events reflect God's usual way of working and supernatural ones his unusual way of working. God designed sexual intercourse as the normal way for human beings to have children—but to deny that he can overrule this if he chooses to do so is a combination of arrogance and ignorance. As the angel told Mary when announcing that she would conceive Jesus while still a virgin, *Nothing will be impossible with God* (Luke 1:37).

The American journalist Larry King wrote a book entitled *How to talk to Anyone, Anytime, Anywhere*. When he was asked who in all of history he would most like to interview he replied, 'Jesus Christ.' In reply to the question, 'And what would you like to ask him?', King said, 'I would like to ask him if he was indeed virgin-born. The answer would define history for me.' King was right in assessing the implications of such an event, and in the light of the biblical evidence there is no need to guess how Jesus would have responded.

Why Jesus? Because nobody else in human history was born of a virgin who had never been impregnated by male sperm.

3 Perfect Ten

Before the 1976 Summer Olympics in Montreal, the scoreboard manufacturer Omega SA asked the organizers whether four digits would be necessary for recording competitors' scores in the gymnastics events. In reply, they were told that three digits would be sufficient as a perfect 10 was not possible. Yet when the Games took place, a fourteen-year-old Romanian gymnast Nadia Comaneci not only won three gold medals but stunned the world of athletics by being awarded a perfect 10 on the uneven bars, then repeating the ultimate score in six further events. She instantly shot to fame and was elected Associated Press Athlete of the Year. In her native Romania she was awarded the title 'Hero of Socialist Labour.' Other national and international awards followed and at a 1999 ceremony in Vienna, Austria she was elected 'Athlete of the Century'.

Hers is a remarkable story, but her 'perfect 10' days in the sporting world have long since passed.

A 'perfect 10' in gymnastics is an amazing achievement, and very few other athletes have succeeded since Nadia Comaneci—but a 'perfect 10' in life as a whole is another matter altogether

The very idea of a perfect person seems beyond human imagination. Even the most exotic fictional figures are flawed in one way or another. None of the mythical Roman and Greek gods were said to be perfect, in spite of the phenomenal powers that were claimed for them. Countless books, magazines, films and other media platforms feature heroes and heroines with mind-blowing personalities, powers and performances, but none is absolutely perfect. It seems that we are incapable of creating anyone who scores a 'perfect 10'. Yet Jesus did—and the evidence is overwhelming.

The exception

The first piece of evidence for this comes from his enemies, a surprising source! In the course of a high-octane exchange with them (which included them accusing him of being demon-possessed) he asked them, *Which one of you convicts me of sin?* (John 8:46). He was speaking to people with finely-tuned antenna when it came to moral and ethical issues, but nobody had a word to say, and their silence says a lot.

Towards the end of his life, several significant people underlined the quality of his character. Judas Iscariot (who at one time had seemed to be a genuine follower) eventually betrayed Jesus to religious authorities who were plotting to have him killed, but he later confessed, *I have sinned by betraying innocent blood* (Matthew 27:4). Judas had been in

Jesus' company for three years and was therefore in a good position to assess his character. While Jesus was on trial (we will look closely at this in the next chapter) the Roman governor's wife had an extraordinary dream, and as a result she warned her husband, *Have nothing to do with that righteous man* (Matthew 27:19). A criminal put on trial at the same time as Jesus told a fellow criminal that they deserved to be executed, then said of Jesus, *… but this man has done nothing wrong* (Luke 23:41). Finally, a Roman army officer in charge of carrying out the court's sentence said of Jesus, *Certainly this man was innocent!* (Luke 23:47).

Sceptics may think that these testimonies fall far short of stating that Jesus was perfect, but they fit in with even stronger statements elsewhere in the New Testament. One of the strongest comes from Saul of Tarsus, a Jewish fundamentalist who was so incensed at what Jesus taught that he set out on a search and destroy mission against the early Christians. At one stage we find him *breathing threats and murder* (Acts 9:1) against Jesus' followers, yet later this brilliant, highly educated and powerful man made a 180-degree turn and put in writing his conviction that Jesus *knew no sin* (2 Corinthians 5:21). When he abandoned his anti-Christian crusade and began to promote Christianity, Saul (whose name had by then been changed to Paul) was flogged, tortured, imprisoned, stoned, suffered *countless beatings* and was *often near death* (2 Corinthians 11:23) yet nothing shook him from his conviction that Jesus had no sin of any kind.

The writer of another New Testament book was equally clear about Jesus' character. He wrote that he was *without sin* (Hebrews 4:15), elaborated by saying that he was *holy, innocent, unstained, separated from sinners* (Hebrews 7:26), then capped it all by saying that Jesus *offered himself without blemish to God* (Hebrews 9:14).

Early in his public ministry Jesus chose twelve disciples as his original followers. From these he picked three men—Peter, James and John—as an inner circle and their testimony is unanimous. They had been with Jesus 24/7 for about three years. They had seen him in public and in private, in times of popularity and of opposition, when he was exhilarated and when he was exhausted; they had over a thousand days in which to come to settled conclusions about his life. Arguments about hearsay evidence or third-hand stories are of no use here. Of this inner circle of three, two testified in writing about Jesus' character. Peter said that Jesus was *without blemish or spot* (1 Peter 1:19), adding that he *committed no sin, neither was deceit found in his mouth* (1 Peter 2:22). As 'no sin' covers everything, there may be more to the extra words than meets the eye. Peter had a bad track record as far as speech was concerned (including bragging and lying) but saw something very different in Jesus and was clearly impressed by the purity and integrity of everything he said.

What makes John's testimony particularly important is that five times he described himself as the disciple *whom Jesus loved* (e.g. John 13:23). As Jesus loved all of his disciples (see John 13:34) this must refer to a particularly close relationship; it certainly meant one that gave John close up and personal opportunities to assess his character. Reflecting on this, John could not have been clearer: *In him there is no sin* (1 John 3:5).

The next piece of evidence is one of the most remarkable: Jesus himself claimed to be perfect. Anybody making that kind of claim today would be written off as a deluded bighead or worse. In the Bible and elsewhere we find the finest of people confessing their failures, not boasting about their moral victories. Israel's King David was one of the greatest men in the Old Testament, yet at one point we find him confessing, *I have sinned greatly in what I have done* (2 Samuel 24:10). Isaiah was among the greatest of the prophets, yet admitted, *I am a man of unclean lips* (Isaiah 6:5). Job was held in the highest esteem, yet cried out, *I despise myself, and repent in dust and ashes* (Job 42:6).

One of the most influential figures since Bible times was the fourth-century Christian leader Augustine, and in his famous book *The Confessions* he said, 'I will now call to mind my past foulness, and the carnal corruptions of my soul.' John Bunyan, who wrote the spiritual masterpiece *Pilgrim's Progress*, called his autobiography *Grace Abounding to the Chief of Sinners*. In the eighteenth century John Wesley's preaching changed the face of England, yet on his deathbed his own assessment was 'I the chief of sinners am.' Wesley's contemporary George Whitefield has been called 'the greatest preacher that England has ever produced', but confessed himself as 'fighting with my corruptions'.

Yet when we look at Jesus the picture is totally different, because he showed no consciousness whatever of personal sin. In the first place, he said quite openly of his relationship with God, *I always do the things that are pleasing to him* (John 8:29). Do you know of anyone else whose life would back up that kind of claim? Secondly, Jesus asserted his innocence by separating himself from his hearers when speaking about sin. When teaching his followers about God answering prayer, he said, *If you, then, who are evil, know how to give good gifts to your children ...* (Matthew 7:11). Why did he say *you who are evil*, not *we who are evil*? There can be only one explanation: he believed that whereas everyone else's life was tainted by sin, his was not. When he taught his disciples what we now call 'the Lord's Prayer' he introduced it by saying, *Pray then like this* (Matthew 6:9). Why did he not say, 'This is how we should pray?'? The answer is obvious: 'the Lord's Prayer' includes the petition, *Forgive us our debts* [our sins] (Matthew 6:12) and Jesus never needed to use those words. He constantly impressed on people the need for them to ask for God's forgiveness, but there is no record of him doing so.

Thirdly, Jesus claimed complete mastery over temptation. Referring to the devil as t*he ruler of this world* he added, *He has no claim on me* (John 14:30), meaning that there was no weakness in him that the devil could exploit. Although the devil threw everything at him, he remained totally unscathed and unstained. He never blushed with shame, never had a guilty conscience, never regretted anything he did, never made a wrong judgement, and never needed to apologize.

The final piece of evidence about the perfection of Jesus is the strongest of all: God said so. Twice during the earthly life of Jesus God spoke from heaven with a voice that could be heard on earth, and each time it was to confirm that Jesus was flawless. On the first occasion, God spoke directly to Jesus and told him, *You are my beloved Son, with you I am well pleased* (Luke 3:22). On the second occasion God spoke to the 'inner circle' of Peter, James and John and told them, *This is my beloved Son, with whom I am well pleased* (Matthew 17:5). What is striking about these statements is that they are the exact opposite of God's verdict on the rest of the human race, which is that *all have sinned and fall short of the glory of God* (Romans 3:23). Yet God said that with Jesus he was 'well pleased', completely satisfied with him. He was delighted in him because he was fulfilling God's plan for his life, and doing so to perfection, without a single flaw or shortcoming of any kind.

One of us

Because we are incapable of imagining a perfect person, some people think that Jesus was not truly human, but that ignores a massive amount of evidence proving that Jesus was fully, truly and totally human. We find him called a 'child' (Matthew 2:11), then a 'boy' (Luke 2:43), then a 'man' (1 Timothy 2:5). He experienced all the normal stages of physical development—he *increased in wisdom and in stature* (Luke 2:52). He had to be taught to stand, to walk, to speak, to write, to feed and to dress himself. His hair grew, his muscles expanded, his voice broke and he passed through puberty into manhood. He needed to eat and drink; there were times when *he became hungry* (Matthew 21:18) and is recorded as calling out, *I thirst* (John 19:28). After a long day's travel he was *wearied ... from his journey* (John 4:6). In the middle of a very demanding day we find him 'asleep' (Matthew 8:24). He did not have a halo or wings. There is no evidence that he was remarkably tall or that he had any other outstanding physical features; you would not have picked him out in a crowd.

He had a perfectly normal emotional life. He called his followers 'friends' (John 15:15) and other people he 'loved' (John 11:5). When a close friend died he was *deeply moved in his spirit* and *wept* (John 11:33, 35). There are marks of genuine humour in several of the stories he told, and when his disciples reported their successes to him he 'rejoiced' (Luke 10:21). He had great sympathy for those in need. When he sensed that people were being harassed by religious rigmarole, *he had compassion for them* (Matthew 9:36). As he approached his death: he *began to be greatly distressed and troubled* and told his disciples, *My soul is very sorrowful* (Mark 14:33-34). The exact words used suggest a wide range of emotions, including shock, fear, confusion, distress, agitation, mental agony, spiritual pain, despondency and horror. A robot could do none of those things.

His humanity also showed through in his spiritual life. He would often *withdraw to desolate places and pray* (Luke 5:16). He regularly attended public worship; *as was his custom, he went to the synagogue on the Sabbath day* (Luke 4:16). We know that he read and studied the Old Testament (the only part of the Bible then written) as he was constantly quoting it from memory, and he often challenged his critics with phrases like *Have you never read in the Scriptures ...?* (Matthew 21:42). Yet perhaps the strongest evidence of Jesus' humanity is that he was tempted to sin. In one horrendous episode he faced Satan head-on *for forty days* (Luke 4:2), and when that was over Satan only left him alone *until an opportune time* (Luke 4:13). Later in the New Testament we are told that in the course of his life he was *in every respect ... tempted as we are'* yet, as the writer adds, was *'without sin* (Hebrews 4:15).

As well as underlining his perfection, the evidence we have pulled together in this chapter rules out the possibility that we can downgrade him to being merely a very good person, or the best person who ever lived, because nobody with any integrity would claim to be perfect (as Jesus did) if he was not.

Why Jesus? Because nobody else in human history has ever been morally, ethically and spiritually flawless.

4 The voluntary victim

In all of human history Jesus has been the only exception to the rule that a person's death is ultimately a tragedy—and the way in which he died was unusual to say the least. He had only three years of public life, and early on in his brief career he ran into mounting opposition. As his reputation grew, some in the nation's religious establishment monitored his every move and soon began gunning for him in a serious way, eventually getting others to join them in making plans *to put him to death* (John 11:53). But why should they want to kill someone who *went about doing good* (Acts 10:38) all over the country? It is not difficult to pinpoint three particular reasons.

The first was that his claim to be the Messiah prophesied in the Old Testament threatened to undermine their authority, as they taught that Messiah had not yet come.

The second was that the amazing miracles he performed attracted huge crowds of people, many of whom were beginning to believe that his claim to be the great deliverer God had promised was valid; this was a growing threat to their position.

The third was that his message flatly contradicted theirs. They taught that the way to get right with God was to obey not only the Ten Commandments laid down in the Old Testament but masses of rules and regulations they had added to these. Jesus openly condemned them for this as it saddled people with *burdens hard to bear* (Luke 11:46). He also directly opposed their core message by teaching that God could not be palmed off with ceremonial religion, or by keeping man-made rules, but that getting right with God was a matter of responding in faith to his love and grace.

This was the last straw as far as the religious authorities were concerned. They moved in for the kill by persuading one of Jesus' followers to betray him for *thirty pieces of silver* (Matthew 26:15)—the average price of a slave in Old Testament times. They then hauled Jesus before both Jewish (religious) and Roman (civil) courts, breaking several laws in the process. Even perjured evidence *by many false witnesses* (Matthew 26:60) failed to prove him guilty of any of the charges brought against him, but at the final trial so much pressure was put on the Roman governor Pontius Pilate that he *delivered him to be crucified* (Mark 15:15). Soldiers then stripped Jesus naked, spat on him, dressed him up to look like a caricature of a king, kneeled before him in mock worship, and led him away to be executed in public.

Crucifixion was a barbaric method of execution forbidden by Jewish law but practised by Romans and others to punish the lowest classes of criminals. It was considered the most shameful and disgraceful way to die, and Roman citizens were usually exempt from it unless they were found guilty of high treason or some other major offence against the state. Victims of crucifixion were sometimes left hanging on a huge wooden cross for days, their bodies exposed to wild animals, insects and birds until they died, often of exposure, trauma, blood loss or heart failure.

Jesus was pronounced dead about six hours after he was nailed to the cross, but this takes nothing away from the disgusting brutality or appalling agony involved in his death. Now comes an amazing fact we dare not miss: the Bible speaks of his death not as something that happened to him against his will, but as something he was instrumental in bringing about. It was not an accident, nor was it a catastrophe, bringing a sudden end to his life before he could add to his achievements. Nor does the Bible teach that he threw his life away by committing suicide. Instead, about a year before he died he anticipated his death by calling it something *he was about to accomplish* (Luke 9:31).

This was exactly how Jesus foresaw his death. Time and again he had warned his followers that they should expect the worst, and that his enemies would *mock him and spit on him, and flog him and kill him* (Mark 10:33-34). Yet he went even further and spoke of his death as being the climax of his life rather than merely its conclusion. When he was capturing the headlines at the beginning of his time in the public eye he knew that his popularity would not define his life; instead, he said, *My hour has not yet come* (John 2:4). Then, a few days before his death, his tone changed and he told two of his friends, *The hour has come*, and underlined this by adding, *... for this purpose I have come to this hour*

(John 12:23, 27). Finally, on the night of his arrest he prayed, *Father, the hour has come* (John 17:1).

Within a few hours he would be executed, but he saw his death not as a tragedy but as a triumph. His death would not conclude his purpose for coming into the world, it would crown it. His death clinched the meaning of his life, so that the greatest thing Jesus did on earth was not to perform miracles, or to live a perfect life, or to give unsurpassed teaching, but to die! He made this clear when a few hours before his death he anticipated it by telling God, *I glorified you on earth, having accomplished the work that you gave me to do* (John 17:4). To discover what that 'work' was we need to take a close look at death in general and a closer look at the death of Jesus in particular.

Why die?

Death is a fact of life—and the only certain fact. 'Is there life after death?' is a question many people ask; 'Is there death after life?' is a question nobody asks, because we all know the answer and we have no choice in the matter. Advances in medical science have virtually eliminated some diseases and can now prolong life in a way that would have been impossible even a few years ago, yet even the finest medical expertise can only postpone the inevitable. The whole world is a hospital, and every person in it a terminal patient; as the Bible bluntly puts it, *It is appointed for man to die* (Hebrews 9:27). Death is an appointment we have no need to make, and one we can do nothing to avoid.

The big question to ask is 'Why?' Why is it that every human being, of whatever race, colour or creed, and whatever their resources, abilities, influence or power, eventually falls victim to what the Bible calls *the king of terrors* (Job 18:14)? There are just four ways of dying: execution (by one method or another), suicide, accident and what we call 'natural causes'. Yet that does nothing to explain death, nor does whatever is written in the 'Cause of Death' column on a death certificate. The real explanation for human mortality is written in the Bible, and is based on the fact that the basic meaning of 'death' is not termination but separation. Physical death is the separation of the soul from the body, while spiritual death is the separation of the soul from God. When we grasp this, we can begin to understand when and why death first invaded human life and why it is inescapable.

God created man as a physical, moral and spiritual reality, stamped with his Creator's character, and for some time (we are given no time frame) he lived in perfect harmony with God and with all of creation. Yet this perfect state of affairs was subject to one condition—man's total and unqualified obedience, linked to God's warning that were he to ignore that condition *you shall surely die* (Genesis 2:17). This was a straightforward test of man's willingness to do what God said simply because God said it—and man failed the test. The result was catastrophic. The moment he disobeyed he died spiritually, his relationship with God fatally smashed. For the first time he knew what it was to feel guilty, ashamed and afraid, and from that moment his body became subject to disease, decay and physical death.

The Bible crystallizes this catastrophe by saying, *Sin came into the world through one man, and death through sin* (Romans 5:12). Man's nature was no longer perfect, but was corrupted by sin, and *from* that moment depravity and corruption were built into human nature just as surely as genes and chromosomes are built into our genetic make-up. King David of Israel, one of the greatest men in the Old Testament, got it absolutely right when he said, *I was brought forth in iniquity, and in sin did my mother conceive me* (Psalm 51:5). This built-in bias is sometimes called 'original sin', and this is what leads not only to all the acts of sin which pollute and ruin our lives but to the inevitable penalty they incur. The fact that we die physically endorses the fact that by nature we are dead spiritually.

The Bible is so insistent on this that it speaks of *the law of sin and death* (Romans 8:2). This law is as fixed and fundamental as the law of gravity. Death is God's righteous and inevitable punishment of human sin. Before man sinned, death was impossible; since he sinned, it is inevitable, and not one single sin can ever avoid death. What is more, the Bible teaches that a person still separated from God by sin at the end of life will suffer *the punishment of eternal destruction, away from the presence of the Lord and from the glory of his might* (2 Thessalonians 1:9). The Bible's most common word for this is 'hell', the ultimate penalty for sin.

No amount of ducking and diving can water this down, but its truth means that the death of Jesus presents us with a conundrum to which there seems to be no obvious answer. As Jesus was not only innocent of the crimes with which he was charged, but had no sin of any kind, and as death is the result of sin, it had no claim on him. Yet Jesus, whose life was perfect, volunteered to submit to the law of sin and death. Why did he do this, deliberately making himself the victim of the greatest miscarriage of justice the world has ever known? In fact, his is the only voluntary death in human history. Not even those who lose their lives trying to rescue others, or military personnel killed in battle, or others who die acting bravely against overwhelming odds, or people who commit suicide, choose to die. In the first three cases, the most they do is to put their lives at risk, while those who commit suicide merely choose the day, the time, the place and the method of their death; dying is not optional; it is inevitable.

Jesus did have an option—and he chose to die. At one point he said, *No one takes [my life] from me, but I lay it down of my own accord* (John 10:18). His meaning could not have been clearer. He would not merely risk his life, but deliberately give it up. At the very moment he died he *cried out again with a loud voice and yielded up his spirit* (Matthew 27:50). Before mechanical ventilators came into use, death was said to be when the heart stopped beating, but this definition could produce tricky situations. Whatever the medical definitions of the exact moment of death, the precise truth is that death comes when the spirit leaves the body. This fits in perfectly with what we see when a person dies. Sometimes the spirit leaves peacefully, while the person concerned is asleep, but sometimes the end is very different

The death of Jesus was certainly different. There was no wrenching of the spirit from the flesh; instead, Jesus 'yielded up his spirit'. The literal meaning of 'yielded up' is 'sent it away', like an employer telling a member of staff to leave work. If a man could prevent the spirit leaving the body, he could make himself immortal; if he could dismiss his spirit by an act of the will, suicide would be simple and serene. Yet Jesus is the exception to the rule. He deliberately, clearly and intelligently dismissed his spirit. He was not drugged (he refused the crude anaesthetic offered to him), and he still had the strength to cry out 'with a loud voice'. He had complete authority over the moment of his death. He died not only by crucifixion, but by choice.

The substitute

Yet this still leaves the major question unanswered: how could he have died if death results from sin and he never sinned? The Bible's answer to that question is amazing: he died on behalf of others and in their place. However stunning that may seem, the Bible's evidence is clear and consistent: *While we were still sinners, Christ died for us* (Romans 5:8); *For our sake [God] made him to be sin who knew no sin* (2 Corinthians 5:21); he *died for us* (1 Thessalonians 5:10); *He himself bore our sins in his body on the tree* (1 Peter 2:24); *He laid down his life for us* (1 John 3:16). This truth is underlined so often that if we removed every direct or indirect reference to it the New Testament would be in shreds.

Many people vaguely accept that Jesus died on behalf of others, but not that he died in their place. There is a difference! Dying on our behalf could mean that he set us an example of how to face the brutal opposition of our enemies. He certainly did that, and the way he did so is an uncomfortable challenge in a world where people's normal reaction is not submission but assertion, not just to get angry but to get even. But this is far from the main thing we see in the death of Jesus; in fact, there is virtually no other place in the New Testament where his suffering and death are said to be an example. This is not surprising, because even his matchless example could do nothing to deal with our greatest problem—the sin that separates us from God.

We can see that the death of Jesus had a special significance when we notice that at one point he cried out, *My God, my God, why have you forsaken me?* (Matthew 27:46). Only hours before, when his closest friends were about to desert him, he had assured them, *I am not alone, for the Father is with me* (John 16:32). Yet in his dying moments that assurance was gone and he seemed to say exactly the opposite. Why? True Christian believers often have a joyful sense of God's presence as they die, yet for Jesus exactly the opposite was true, and his closing moments were full of anguish. Thousands of Christian martyrs have faced their closing moments with amazing joy, yet Jesus did the opposite. The explanation is that on the cross he was experiencing not merely physical death but spiritual death. As the Bible puts it, *For our sake* [God] *made him to be sin who knew no sin* (2 Corinthians 5:21).

God has zero tolerance of sin, and his holiness demands that all sin be punished. When Jesus became accountable for the sins of others he was punished as though he had committed them, and he bore that punishment in both his body and his spirit. When Jesus cried that he had been forsaken by God the Father, it did not mean that the Father was not there (as God is always everywhere), but that he was not there to strengthen, comfort and bless him. Instead, in his righteous anger against sin, God the Father deserted, rejected and punished him.

This takes us to the very heart of why Jesus died and what his death accomplished for those whose place he took, and we see it best through the eyes of some of those who first realized what had happened. One writes that Jesus died *the righteous for the unrighteous, that he might bring us to God* (1 Peter 3:18). In his perfect life Jesus met all the demands of

God's holy law. In his death he paid in full the penalty demanded by that law; and he did both on behalf of others who deserved to pay it. One of the Bible's big words for being brought back into a living relationship with God is 'justification', and the apostle Paul wrote, *We have now been justified by his blood* (Romans 5:9). To be justified means to be made right with God, and those in whose place Jesus shed his blood are said to be perfectly holy in God's sight, as the penalty for all of their sin was paid for by the one who took their place. Paul assured early Christians that whatever their past they were now, *holy and blameless and above reproach before* [God] (Colossians 1:21-22). God does not pronounce guilty people to be innocent (which would be untrue) but—amazingly—he accepts the death of Jesus in their place. God declares them righteous on the basis of the life and death of his Son, who took their place and acted on their behalf.

The Bible says that by nature our minds are *hostile to God* (Romans 8:7). Left to ourselves we are in self-centred rebellion against our Maker, preferring to determine our own lifestyle. This exposes us to God's holy anger, which we can do nothing to prevent. Yet God (the innocent party) has taken the initiative and done something astonishing to enable us (the guilty party) to be at peace with him by dealing with the root cause of the rift—human sin. In the death of Jesus, God not only punished human sin but also satisfied his own righteous judgement, and in this way removed the barrier separating him from sinners. This is why the apostle Paul writes, *While we were enemies we were reconciled to God by the death of his Son* (Romans 5:10) and tells early Christians, *You who once were far off have been brought near by the blood of Christ* (Ephesians 2:13).

At the precise moment Jesus died, God provided an amazing visual aid to illustrate this. The temple in Jerusalem was the focal point of the nation's worship. In it, a richly-embroidered veil or curtain separated the 'Holy Place' from the 'Most Holy Place', the inner sanctuary that represented God's presence. As Jesus drew his last breath, *The curtain of the temple was torn in two, from top to bottom* (Matthew 27:51). No human being was responsible for this. It was nothing less than a miracle, a God-given sign that whereas under the old religious system the high priest alone could enter the symbolic presence of God (and then only once a year) the death of Jesus had removed the sin barrier between God and man. Now, all those for whom he died could be reconciled to God without any religious trappings. Later, a first-century Christian wrote, *We have confidence to enter the holy places by the blood of Jesus, by the new and living way that he opened for us through the curtain, that is, through his flesh* (Hebrews 10:19-20). In the death of Jesus the barrier separating sinful men from a holy God was torn apart. In the death of Jesus the guilt and condemnation of those in whose place he died were removed for ever. Paul told Christians in Ephesus that Jesus had died in their place so that he might *reconcile us both to God ... through the cross, thereby killing the hostility* (Ephesians 2:16), and elsewhere wrote, *We have peace with God through our Lord Jesus Christ* (Romans 5:1).

Another picture of man without God is one that shows him not only to be guilty, but to be in debt—and Jesus dealt with that, too, paying man's debt on the cross. This enables God to forgive the debtor in whose place Jesus died from both his guilt and his indebtedness, cutting him loose from its burden and setting him free to lead a new life. Paul wrote, *In* [Jesus Christ] *we have redemption through his blood, the forgiveness of our trespasses* (Ephesians 1:7). Jesus was more than an example, he was a substitute, taking the place of those who were spiritually bankrupt and could do nothing to pay their appalling debt. Many people think of God only as a God of love, always on hand to help when things go wrong, and bound in the end to forgive everybody's sins and receive them into heaven for ever, but this idea is fatally misleading. The Bible certainly tells us that *God is love* (1 John 4:8), but also that he is *majestic in holiness* (Exodus 15:11) and that *the wrath of God is revealed from heaven against all ungodliness and unrighteousness of men* (Romans 1:18). Only if the debt of sin is paid can God's rightful anger be removed; in the death of Jesus it was, providing the only way in which God could be satisfied and man could be saved.

In the death of Jesus two amazing things come to light. The first is God's perfect justice. It is often said that there is no such thing as perfect justice—but there is. The Bible says of God that *all his ways are justice* (Deuteronomy 32:4), which means that every sin ever committed in the whole of human history must be punished. God's very character is at stake here. The second is God's amazing love. As the Bible puts it, *God shows his love for us in that while we were still sinners, Christ died for us* (Romans 5:8). You will never read anything more astonishing than this! By nature and by choice we are *hostile to God* (Romans 8:7), deliberate rebels against his authority and determined to choose our own standards and lifestyle. Yet in spite of this, God's love for us is so amazing that in order to rescue us from the appalling penalty our sin deserves he d*id not spare his own Son but gave him up for us all* (Romans 8:32). No human love can possibly match or illustrate this; *Christ died for the ungodly* (Romans 5:6) is simply unique. Here is another statement that countless people rate as the best overall summary of this tremendous truth:

> *For God so loved the world, that he gave his only*
> *Son, that whoever believes in him should not perish*
> *but have eternal life* (John 3:16).

Why Jesus? Because nobody else in human history chose to die, then deliberately did so in the place of others and on their behalf, taking the punishment they deserved and paying the debt they owed.

5 Man Alive!

Death bothers people, not least because nobody knows what it is like to experience it personally. We are creatures of comfort, and always feel more secure going into familiar situations. Death is different, because we know nothing about it at first hand. Even if we have been intimately involved in someone else's dying (I was holding my stepmother's hand when she died) we have not shared in that person's death. As we saw in Chapter 4, the subject raises a question to which most people would like to have a clear answer: is there life after death?

The idea that death is not only the end of life but the end of the person concerned goes back a long way, but is perhaps best summed up by the philosopher who said, 'When I die I shall rot.' Not everybody signs up to these pessimistic prophecies, and many try to skirt around the issue of whether there is life after death by claiming, 'Nobody has ever come back to tell us.' This seems a reasonable line to take—but history is against it, because someone has ...

Jesus died at about 3pm on a Friday. His followers wanted to make sure that he was buried before 6.00pm, when the Jewish Sabbath began, so they asked Pilate to follow the usual procedure and have Jesus' legs broken to confirm that he was dead. When the Roman soldiers went to do this they found that he was already dead and that there was therefore no need to break his legs, but to make absolutely sure one of the soldiers *pierced his side with a spear* (John 19:34). One of Jesus' friends, Joseph of Arimathea, then got permission to take the body down from the cross, and another man helped him to carry it away to a nearby garden and place it in a tomb Joseph had earmarked for his own burial. After laying the body in the tomb they embalmed it, wrapping it in a tightly wound shroud layered with a sticky mixture of myrrh and aloes *about seventy-five pounds in weight* (John 19:39). Two other friends of Jesus were there at the time and *saw the tomb and how his body was laid* (Luke 23:55). We can easily imagine these four mourners leaving the garden that evening, sick with sorrow that they would never see Jesus again.

By Sunday morning the body had gone! At least five people who visited the tomb, including Peter, one of Jesus' inner circle, confirmed this. There is no contemporary record of anybody denying the fact, and some 2,000 years later nobody has produced any credible indication that these people were lying. On the other hand, all the evidence points to a sensational reason for the empty tomb—Jesus came back to life!

The strongest contemporary evidence is that six independent witnesses tell of him appearing to varying numbers of people on eleven separate occasions over a period of forty days. Here is the record:

• Within three days of his burial Jesus *appeared first to Mary Magdalene, from whom he had cast out seven demons* (Mark 16:9).

• As a group of women were hurrying back to Jerusalem to tell the disciples about the empty tomb and what the angel had told them, *Jesus met them* (Matthew 28:9).

• Later that day, as two of Jesus' followers were walking to Emmaus, a village about two miles from Jerusalem, *Jesus himself drew near and went with them* (Luke 24:15).

• After having an evening meal with Jesus, they rushed back to Jerusalem to tell the disciples, but before they could get their story out they were told, *The Lord has risen indeed, and has appeared to Simon!* [i.e. Peter] (Luke 24:34).

• While they were comparing notes about these appearances *Jesus himself stood among them, and said to them, "Peace to you!"* (Luke 24:36).

• A week later, when the disciples were in hiding for fear of being arrested, *Jesus came and stood among them and said, "Peace be with you"* (John 20:26).

• Later, *Jesus revealed himself again to the disciples by the Sea of Tiberias* (John 21:1).

• There was one occasion when Jesus *appeared to more than five hundred brothers [i.e. Christian believers] at one time* (1 Corinthians 15:6).

• He also *appeared to James, then to all the apostles* (1 Corinthians 15:7).

• He appeared to eleven disciples when they were on a hillside in Galilee, and *when they saw him they worshipped him* (Matthew 28:17).

• Seven weeks after his resurrection Jesus gathered his followers together and *led them out as far as Bethany*, where, after giving them some final instructions, *he parted from them and was carried up into heaven* (Luke 24:50-51).

This is the immediate evidence that Jesus rose from the dead, and it was backed up by what followed. Soon after his final appearance to them this handful of men became a dynamic and fearless band of believers prepared to face persecution, imprisonment and execution rather than deny their convictions. When they were threatened with this kind of treatment unless they stopped preaching the resurrection of Jesus, they replied, *We must obey God rather than men* (Acts 5:29) and carried on preaching.

The empty tomb is not proof that Jesus rose from the dead, but to believe that the disciples would put their own lives on the line by preaching that Jesus was alive when they knew that his body was still in the grave is clutching at very thin straws. People may sometimes be willing to die for something they believe to be true (and countless terrorists and fanatics do so), but nobody is prepared to die for something they know to be false.

When their inspirational leader was arrested, tortured and executed, his followers ran away like frightened rabbits; yet soon afterwards they were like roaring lions, prepared to stake their lives on his resurrection. Peter, for example, their chief spokesman, had not only deserted Jesus when the chips were down, but had denied that he even knew him, yet when he and John were arrested and brought before the authorities for preaching the resurrection he never flinched, leaving his accusers *astonished* at *the boldness of Peter and John* (Acts 4:13). The only explanation for the change from cowardice to courage is that they were telling the truth.

The same change came over all the others. No longer afraid of what might happen to them, they staked their lives on one thing: Jesus was alive. Nothing - neither ridicule, persecution, imprisonment nor even the threat of execution - could stop them. They were transformed, radiant and irresistible. Fear had given way to faith, despair to delight and paralysis to power.

After I had spoken at The University of Cape Town, South Africa, an atheist bombarded me with questions. As I was being called away to another engagement, I asked him one of my own: 'What do you think of Jesus Christ?' I have never forgotten his reply: 'I am not sure, but I do know this: everything depends on whether or not he rose from the dead.' He was spot on—in more ways than he may have realized. In the first place the writers of the New Testament unanimously say Jesus came back to life, and they never refer to it as a myth or legend, but always as an historical event. One of them says that Jesus *presented himself alive ... by many proofs* (Acts 1:3). Secondly, Jesus not only promised his followers that he would come back to life but even told them exactly how long after his burial this would happen: *After three days I will rise* (Matthew 27:63). Predicting his death would have been easy. Predicting that he would come back from the dead was very different. It would mean that if this never happened he was either a fool or a deluded liar - and we saw in Chapter 3 that he was neither.

Theories

Many have tried to come up with alternative theories as to why Jesus' tomb was empty three days after he was buried. One of the most radical is to say that he never died. The so-called Swoon Theory suggests that although he had been beaten and scourged, pinned by his hands and feet to a cross for six hours, ripped open by a soldier's spear, then certified as dead by the leader of the execution squad, he had merely passed out. This asks us to believe that neither of the men who took his body down from the cross and placed it in a tomb noticed any sign of life. What is more, at some time after the tomb was sealed with a huge rock, Jesus somehow wriggled out of his embalming shroud, pushed the massive rock away, overpowered the Roman guards posted there to prevent any trouble, then made his way into the city (presumably naked, as the burial shroud was left behind) and deliberately fooled his disciples into believing that he had conquered death. This would mean that after a lifetime during which he was without sin his moral DNA did a 180-degree turn and he deliberately hoodwinked his followers into believing a lie, knowing that if they swallowed his story they would be ruthlessly persecuted. As conspiracy theories go, this one may be the most ridiculous of all.

Another theory says that every one of Jesus' followers who went to visit his burial place on that Sunday went to the wrong tomb. It is just possible that the first visitors, who went *at early dawn* (Luke 24:1) might initially have lost their way in the semi-darkness, but at least five others went to the garden later in the day; did they make the same mistake in broad daylight? Even if we go along with the idea that they all did, why did nobody ask Joseph? As he had bought the tomb in the first place, he would certainly have known where it was, and as he had very recently laid Jesus' body there he was obviously not suffering from an outbreak of amnesia.

Four other theories point to the body having been removed from the grave and taken somewhere else. The first suggests that it was stolen by a person or persons unknown. As with some of the other theories, this one runs up against the armed Roman guard that would have needed to be overpowered. It is just as difficult to invent a motive for the robbers. Far from being a wealthy man, Jesus was exactly the opposite (at one point he had to borrow a coin to give an illustration) so they would not have heard that a rich man had insisted on having expensive possessions buried with him. One other thing: as the grave-clothes were left in the tomb, it would mean that all the robbers removed was a naked corpse. Why would they do this? As Sir Norman Anderson wryly commented, 'A Jew of that period could scarcely be suspected of stealing bodies on behalf of anatomical research!'

The second suggests that the Roman authorities may have removed the body. As they were in charge of the tomb they had a unique opportunity to do this—but why would they? Because the Jewish religious leaders had told Pilate about Jesus prophesying that he would rise from the dead after three days, Pilate had insisted on maximum security at the tomb, not only with an armed guard, but with his own seal fixed to the rock placed over the entrance (tampering with it would have meant execution). What could be gained by dismantling all of this security and moving the body elsewhere? Why would the Romans want the body back? What is more, if the Roman authorities had the body in their own custody they would have produced it as soon as the disciples began preaching that Jesus was alive—and the Christian church would have collapsed on the spot.

The third theory is that the body was removed by the Jewish religious authorities. They would certainly have had a powerful motive to do so, precisely because of Jesus' prophecy that he would rise from the dead on the third day. All they had to do was remove the body and keep it under lock and key for four days. At that point Jesus would be exposed as having been a fool or a liar, and the disciples' claim would have been laughed out of court. Yet when the disciples began preaching the resurrection of Jesus, the Jews had them arrested, imprisoned, flogged and executed. Why did they do this instead of simply producing the body?

The last body-removing suspects are Jesus' own disciples, but this is a pathetic proposition. Firstly, they had no opportunity to do so. The armed Roman guard would have been more than a match for a handful of men who when Jesus was arrested *all left him and fled* (Mark 14:50) and when he was executed hid behind locked doors *for fear of the Jews* (John 20:19), terrified that they might be next on the authorities' hit list. Can we seriously imagine that this panic-stricken rabble suddenly plucked up the courage to go to the tomb, tackle an armed guard and risk the death penalty by breaking the governor's official seal to get inside the tomb, all for the purpose of taking possession of a dead body that was already in the safe keeping of a fellow Christian? If they did, why is there no record of them being charged with such serious offences? Yet there is another reason for rejecting the suggestion that the disciples stole the body. These men had been powerfully influenced by Jesus and their lives had been transformed. As one of them was to write later, a person wanting to enjoy God's blessing on his life should *keep his tongue from evil and his lips from speaking deceit* (1 Peter 3:10). It is inconceivable that men whose moral standards had been elevated to a level they had never known before should now base their entire teaching on a pack of lies they knew they had invented—and risk their own lives into the bargain.

Call Paul

Earlier in the chapter we looked at appearances Jesus made after his resurrection, all of which took place within a period of forty days, but there is one other that is worth examining more closely, the case of Saul (we met him in Chapter 3). He was born in Tarsus, a university town and commercial centre in Mersin Province, Turkey, but at that time the capital city of the Roman province of Cilicia in Asia Minor. His parents were of solid Jewish stock and could trace their ancestry back to the elite Old Testament tribe of Benjamin. After a thoroughly religious education in Tarsus he moved to Jerusalem, where he studied under the great Jewish scholar Gamaliel. While still a student, Saul joined the strictest sect in the Jewish religion becoming a dedicated Pharisee. As such, he accepted the entire Old Testament as God's law and strongly opposed all who took a looser, liberal approach to the ancient text.

When the Christian church came into existence Saul saw it as a direct threat to his Jewish faith. He firmly believed that one day God would send his promised Messiah to fulfil all the Old Testament prophecies and ultimately to set up a perfect and everlasting kingdom, but 400 years had passed since the last of these and there was no sign of him. Then suddenly Jesus burst on the scene and, as we saw in Chapter 1, claimed that he was the promised Messiah and that all these prophecies referred to him. As far as Saul was concerned, this was the tipping point. The idea that a carpenter's son from a small town not even mentioned in the Old Testament, and who had been executed like a common criminal, was God's promised Messiah was more than he could take. Determined to wipe out those who were now worshipping someone he rated as a blasphemous imposter, he set out on a search and destroy mission against all Christians.

Beginning at Jerusalem, he flushed believers out of their homes and had them thrown into prison. Later, armed with arrest warrants from the high priest, he travelled to foreign cities as far away as Damascus, in Syria. Wherever he found Christians he dragged them before local courts, tried to force them to blaspheme, or in his *raging fury* (Acts 26:11) hauled them back to Jerusalem for punishment, which at times meant the death sentence.

Then something amazing happened to Saul. While on his way to Damascus he had a dramatic experience that transformed his life. Writing about it later, he listed some of the people to whom Jesus appeared after his resurrection, then added, *Last of all... he appeared also to me'* (1 Corinthians 15:8). Although this happened long after Jesus had returned to heaven Saul (now Paul) clearly knew that his experience of meeting with him was just as real as those in the eleven other cases listed earlier in this chapter. When people in Corinth questioned his status and authority he had no hesitation in replying, *Am I not an apostle? Have I not seen Jesus our Lord?* (1 Corinthians 9:1).

Claims that Paul and the other professing witnesses were lying can easily be brushed aside. There is not a shred of evidence to support this—and what possible motive could they have had for doing so, when insisting they had seen Jesus alive after death was certain to get them into serious trouble? Paul's experience alone is enough to demolish any charge of dishonesty. He had been a high-profile persecutor of the Christian church, but after his Damascus road experience he became utterly convinced that in attacking the Christian faith he had been fighting not for the truth but against it. He immediately became a passionate preacher of the faith he was once determined to destroy and was eventually to write more about the resurrection of Jesus than any other New Testament writer.

In his own words, his work as an apostle brought him face to face with *danger from my own people, danger from Gentiles, danger in the city, danger in the wilderness, danger at sea, danger from false brothers* as well as having *many a sleepless night* and being *in hunger and thirst, often without food* and *in cold and exposure* (2 Corinthians 11:26-27). Would he have deliberately left himself open to all of this, and eventually be willing to die, for something he knew he had invented? Any competent psychologist would make short work of that idea. People will often lie to get out of trouble, but never to get into it.

The legacy

Today, there are over two billion professing Christians in the world and the number is growing by thousands every day. In spite of its weaknesses, the Christian church has been an immense influence for good throughout the world. In the foundation of schools, hospitals and institutions to care for the homeless and destitute, in spearheading the abolition of the slave trade or improving the conditions of those working in mills and mines or suffering appalling conditions in prisons, no organization has done more. In our day Christians around the world are outstanding examples of caring for the blind and the deaf, the orphaned and the widowed, the poor and the hungry, the deprived and disadvantaged, the homeless and the helpless, the sick and the dying. One historical event has been the dynamic motive driving centuries of this loving, selfless service—the resurrection of Jesus from the dead. If it had never happened it is difficult to explain how the Christian church ever got started. As preacher D. James Kennedy put it: 'The Grand Canyon wasn't caused by an Indian dragging a stick, and the Christian church wasn't created by a myth.'

The evidence for the resurrection of Jesus has convinced many eminent men well qualified to assess the truth and in the judgement of Lord Darling, a former Chief Justice of England, 'There exists such overwhelming evidence, positive and negative, factual and circumstantial, that no intelligent jury could fail to bring in a verdict that the resurrection is true.'

Why Jesus? Because nobody else in human history has risen from the dead and is alive today, transforming people's lives.

6 The invader

The resurrection of Jesus has at least as much contemporary confirmation as any other event that took place around 2,000 years ago. In a document found among his private papers after his death, Lord Lyndhurst, one of the greatest minds in English legal history, wrote, 'I know pretty well what evidence is; and I tell you, such evidence as that for the resurrection has never broken down yet.' We saw earlier in this book that Jesus' conception, life and death were unique; so was his resurrection. We will shortly see why this was the case, but before we do it is worth noting that if it had not happened there would be no way to explain in full any of the following statements:

- Nobody knows the exact date of his birth, but that one event divides the whole of world history into the years labelled 'BC' (before Christ) and 'AD' (from the Latin Anno Domini, meaning 'in the year of the Lord').

• He never wrote a book, but more books have been written about him than anyone else in history. The nearest thing we have to his biography—the Bible's New Testament—has been translated in whole or in part into over 2,500 languages.

• He never painted a picture or composed any poetry or music, but nobody's life and teaching has been the subject of a greater output of songs, plays, poetry, pictures, films, videos and other art forms.

• He never raised an army, but millions of people have laid down their lives in his cause. Credible evidence has been claimed that some 100,000 people are killed every year because of their faith in Jesus Christ.

• Except for one brief period during his childhood, his travels were limited to an area the size of Wales (or the American state of New Jersey) but today his influence is literally worldwide.

• He never spoke to more than a few thousand people at any one time, but today his followers constitute the largest religious grouping the world has ever known.

• His public teaching lasted only three years and was restricted to one tiny country, but today some of the world's radio and television networks are given over exclusively to spreading his words, while purpose-built communication satellites are positioned in space to carry his message around the globe.

• He set foot in only two countries, but one Christian missionary organization claims to fly regularly to more countries than any commercial airline in the world.

• He had no formal education, but thousands of universities, seminaries, colleges and schools have been founded in his name.

• He never owned any property and had to borrow a boat to sail in, a donkey to ride on, and (as we saw earlier) even a coin to use for an illustration, but thousands of buildings all around the world have been built for the sole purpose of teaching his followers and adding to their number.

• In his own lifetime he was relatively unknown outside of his own small country, but in the current edition of Encyclopaedia Britannica the entry on 'Jesus' runs to nearly 30,000 words, while typing 'Jesus' into an internet search engine will produce about 600,000,000 results.

Claims

His resurrection from the dead is the only credible explanation for why these eleven statements are true. It is also a spectacular signpost to the greatest thing the Bible says about him, which is that he *was declared to be the Son of God in power... by his resurrection from the dead* (Romans 1:4). Jesus gave more than a hint of this when he told a well-known religious leader that he had *descended from heaven* (John 3:13). Elsewhere he spoke of his life in heaven *before the world existed* (John 17:5). Jesus was born on a certain date, but he told his hearers that he had always existed; in other words he had a birth but no beginning.

He illustrated this in a conversation with sceptical Jews. At one point they asked him whether he was greater than the Jewish patriarch Abraham (who had died some 2,000 years earlier). In reply Jesus told them, *Before Abraham was, I am* (John 8:58). He was not claiming to be older than Abraham, as he accepted their comment that he was *not yet fifty years old* (John 8:57). He did not even say, 'Before Abraham was born I was', but *Before Abraham was born I am*. What made this so mind-blowing to the sceptics was that *I am* (Exodus 3:14) was one of the names by which God revealed himself in the Old Testament. The name infers eternal, timeless self-existence, something uniquely true of God—yet Jesus had no hesitation in using it about himself. It is important to notice that the Jews had asked him, *Who do you make yourself out to be?* (John 8:53), so the issue was not his age, but his identity. The reply Jesus gave was crystal clear: he claimed to be God. Those who heard him do this *picked up stones to throw at him* (John 8:59). This was the penalty for blasphemy, and as far as they were concerned there could be no greater blasphemy than a creature claiming to be the Creator.

Nor was this a one-off incident. Some time later hostile Jews *picked up stones again to stone him* (John 10:31). When Jesus asked them (tongue in cheek?) which of his miracles had driven them to do this, they replied, *It is not for a good work that we are going to stone you but for blasphemy, because you, being a man, make yourself God* (John 10:32-33). They had not the slightest doubt about what Jesus was saying, and the New Testament is packed with teaching that underlines it. When Richard Dawkins claims, 'There is no good historical evidence that [Jesus] ever thought he was divine' he is tripping blindfold over the truth. C. S. Lewis gets us on the right track when he writes, 'The doctrine of Christ's divinity seems to me not something stuck on which you can unstick, but something that peeps out at every point, so that you would have to unravel the whole web to get rid of it.' We can begin to see this by looking at three other direct claims Jesus made.

The first was when one of his disciples asked for concrete evidence on which to build their faith. They were not philosophers, academics or theologians, but ordinary down-to-earth people, for whom seeing was believing. They had heard Jesus teach about the kingdom of God, the power of God, the love of God, and much more about him; now they wanted something extra, and one of them got straight to the point: *Lord, show us the Father, and it is enough for us* (John 14:8). Jesus had taught them earlier that when praying to God they should call him 'Father', so it is clear what they were asking. Jesus met the challenge head-on: *Have I been with you so long, and you still do not know me, Philip? Whoever has seen me has seen the Father* (John 14:9). Centuries before, God had told Moses that *man shall not see me and live* (Exodus 33:20); now Jesus was saying that he (God the Son) revealed all of God's character and nature that it was possible and necessary for a human being to see and know. As one New Testament writer put it, Jesus *made him known* (John 1:18).

The second claim was made a few hours before his death, when Jesus prayed, *And now, Father, glorify me in your own presence with the glory that I had with you before the world existed* (John 17:5). He was clearly claiming that this shared glory was not given to him at any time in the past but was something he possessed eternally, before the world had even been created. He was addressing God on equal terms.

The third claim was made shortly afterwards, while Jesus was with his disciples in the Garden of Gethsemane and a squad of soldiers (tipped off by the traitor Judas Iscariot) came to arrest him. When Jesus asked them, *Whom do you seek?* they said, *Jesus of Nazareth.* When Jesus replied, *I am he* they *drew back and fell to the ground* (John 18:4-6). Why would they do that? Jesus was emotionally exhausted, unarmed, and offering no resistance, yet when Jesus answered their question in the way he did a whole detachment of armed troops staggered backwards and clattered to the ground. On that performance, they were hardly special services material! Then why did they suddenly keel over? The explanation lies in the phrase Jesus used. Translators have added the word 'he' to round out the sentence, but Jesus said just two words—*ego eimi*. This simply means 'I am' (the divine title we noticed earlier in this chapter) but the majesty and glory of those two words and the way they were spoken literally swept the soldiers off their feet in a spectacular demonstration of the presence and power of God.

Titles

As we read the New Testament we find that time and again Jesus is given names or titles that apply only to God. One dates back to Old Testament times when God's people shied away from making direct references to him by name. They were so reluctant to spell out his sacred name - Yahweh - that they shortened it to four consonants, *yhwh*, and even in that coded form it had to be used very carefully. Other Hebrew words for God included *adonay* and *elohim*, and in the twelfth century it was a combination of the consonants *yhwh* and the vowels from these two words that produced the word 'Jehovah' which is sometimes used of God today.

When the Old Testament was first translated from Hebrew to Greek, the word most commonly chosen to translate *yhwh* and *adonay* was *kyrie*, which our English versions of the Bible almost always translate as 'Lord'. In well over 6,000 cases the word *kyrios* (Lord) is used as a translation or synonym of one or other of the major Old Testament words for God, and to mean that 'the Lord' is the almighty Creator and Sustainer of the universe to whom all men owe unqualified worship and obedience. Yet New Testament writers constantly quote Old Testament statements about 'the Lord' and apply them to Jesus. It is easy to find examples.

The prophet Isaiah called God's people to prepare for a later prophet who would call out, *In the wilderness prepare the way of the Lord* (Isaiah 40:3). Centuries later an itinerant preacher now known as John the Baptist announced himself as *the voice of one crying out in the wilderness, "Make straight the way of the Lord", as the prophet Isaiah said* (John 1:23)—and immediately introduced his listeners to Jesus.

Isaiah also warned that to some people the Lord would be *a stone of offence and a rock of stumbling* (Isaiah 8:14); and over 400 years later the apostle Peter had this prophecy in mind when he described Jesus as *A stone of stumbling, and a rock of offence* (1 Peter 2:8). One of the psalmists said of the Lord, *You laid the foundation of the earth, and the heavens are the work of your hands* (Psalm 102:25); and a New Testament writer said of Jesus, *You, Lord, laid the foundation of the earth in the beginning, and the heavens are the work of your hands* (Hebrews 1:10). Writing of God's power and mercy, the prophet Joel said, *Everyone who calls on the name of the Lord shall be saved* (Joel 2:32); and both Peter (at Acts 2:21) and Paul (at Romans 10:13) quote Joel verbatim when writing about Jesus. But these examples are just the tip of the iceberg, and Paul refers to Jesus as 'Lord' about 200 times.

Another key title is one that was used of Jesus before he was born. As we saw in Chapter 2, an angel told Mary that her child would be *called the Son of the Most High*, and that *of his kingdom there will be no end* (Luke 1:32-33). The description 'Most High' occurs nearly sixty times in the Bible and is used only of God. The angel underlined the news by telling Mary that Jesus would be called *the Son of God* (Luke 1:35). This title was to be used of God over thirty times in the New Testament, including, as we saw earlier in this chapter, Jesus being *declared to be the Son of God in power* Romans 1:14) after his resurrection.

Elsewhere in the New Testament the writers confirm the divine nature of Jesus in the clearest possible way. The apostle Paul calls him *the image of the invisible God* (Colossians 1:15) and says that in him *all the fullness of God was pleased to dwell* (Colossians 1:19). Elsewhere he speaks of *our great God and Saviour, Jesus Christ* (Titus 2:13). Peter writes of *the righteousness of our God and Saviour Jesus Christ* (2 Peter 1:1). John calls him *the true God and eternal life* (1 John 5:20) and the writer of Hebrews describes him as *the radiance of the glory of God and the exact imprint of his nature* (Hebrews 1:3). If these are not telling us that Jesus is God it is difficult to know what they are saying! Having carefully weighed up the biblical evidence, C. S. Lewis came to this conclusion: 'I have to accept that [Jesus] was and is God. God has landed on this enemy-occupied world in human form.'

What if ...?

Imagine a group of people, without knowing that the New Testament existed, getting together to talk about God, religion, faith and life. Somebody asks, 'I wonder what would happen if God became a man? What kind of man would he be?' The others think this is a bizarre idea, but just to open up an interesting discussion they go along with it. Here are some of the answers they might give.

'If God became a man, he would be able to explain the Old Testament.' As we saw earlier in this book, the Old Testament is full of statements such as *The word of the Lord came* (Jeremiah 1:2), so God could obviously give a perfect explanation of what those thirty-nine books said and meant. This is exactly what Jesus did. Over the centuries, countless theologians had put their own spin on Old Testament teaching, sometimes adding rules and regulations of their own, but Jesus brushed all of these aside and often told his hearers, *You have heard that it was said ... but I say to you ...* (Matthew 5:21-22), obviously claiming to know exactly what the Old Testament writers meant. On another occasion he went much further and said that all the Old Testament writings *bear witness about me* (John 5:39), clearly claiming that the key to understanding the Old Testament was to see that it pointed to him.

'If God became a man he would live a perfect life.' The Old Testament says that God is *majestic in holiness* (Exodus 15:11) and *filled with righteousness* (Psalm 48:10)—in other words, that he is perfect. So was Jesus. We saw earlier that although he was tempted in every way that we are he was *without sin* (Hebrews 4:15). The same writer says that Jesus was *holy, innocent, unstained, separated from sinners* (Hebrews 7:26). Elsewhere we are told that he *knew no sin* (2 Corinthians 5:21) and that he was *without blemish or spot* (1 Peter 1:19). His moral life was a mirror image of what we should expect from God himself.

'If God became a man he would know what everybody else was thinking.' The Old Testament tells us that God is *a God of knowledge* (1 Samuel 2:3) and is *perfect in knowledge*

(Job 37:10). The same kind of thing was said of Jesus. He *knew all people* and *knew what was in man* (John 2:24-25). Elsewhere we read of him possessing *all the treasures of wisdom and knowledge* (Colossians 2:3).

'If God became a man he would be unchangeable.' In the Old Testament God himself says, *I the Lord do not change* (Malachi 3:6), while one of the psalmists says of God, *You are the same, and your years have no end* (Psalm 102:27). The same words are applied to Jesus. He is *the same yesterday and today and for ever* (Hebrews 13:8); he is *the Alpha and the Omega, the first and the last, the beginning and the end* (Revelation 22:13).

'If God became a man, he would easily be able to solve any food supply crisis.' God did this in the Old Testament. For years he miraculously sent food overnight to meet the needs of his people as they wandered in the desert after their escape from Egypt (see Exodus 16), while other incidents included supplying the needs of at least 100 men with a few loaves of barley bread (see 2 Kings 4:42-44). Jesus did the same kind of thing. He made five loaves and two fish feed well over 5,000 people in such a way that *they all ate and were satisfied*, with t*welve baskets full* of scraps left over (see Matthew 14:13-21). On another occasion, seven loaves and a few small fish met the needs of over 4,000 people, and the left-overs filled seven baskets (see Matthew 15: 32-37).

'If God became a man he would be able to heal sicknesses whenever he chose to do so.' In the Old Testament, God's power to do this was such that he told his people, *I am the Lord, your healer* (Exodus 15:26). Jesus healed sickness of every kind at will. He healed the blind, the deaf, the dumb the lame, the leprous and the paralyzed—in fact, at one point we find him *healing every disease and every affliction among the people* (Matthew 4:23). His healing power met more than purely physical needs and included delivering *all who were oppressed by the devil* (Acts 10:38). The miracles Jesus performed point clearly to his divine identity.

'If God became a man he could bring the dead back to life.' God did this in Old Testament times. For example, he used the prophet Elijah in bringing a widow's son back to life (see 1 Kings 17:17-24) and the prophet Elisha in restoring life to another child (see 2 Kings 4: 8-37). Jesus performed the same amazing miracle several times. He brought at least three people back to life, including one who had been buried for four days (see Luke 7:11-17; Matthew 9:18-26; John 11:1-44).

'If God became a man he could control the natural elements.' The best-known Old Testament example of this happened when God held back the Red Sea to enable the Israelites to escape from captivity in Egypt (see Exodus 14:1-31). Jesus demonstrated the same control. When he and his disciples were caught in a fierce windstorm on the Sea of Galilee and the disciples (several of them experienced sailors who could read the situation well) thought they were certain to be drowned, Jesus *rebuked the wind and the raging waves, and they ceased, and there was a calm* (Luke 8:24).

At this point, someone might even go so far as to say, 'If God became a man and was somehow put to death, he would come back to life.' This is obviously true, as he is *the eternal God* (Deuteronomy 33:27). Yet this is exactly what Jesus did. As we saw in Chapter 5, he appeared time and again to his followers after his public execution, and *presented himself alive ... by many proofs* (Acts 1:3).

These matches are impressive. If modern profilers were to pull together all the biblical data we have on God, then look for a match among all the 107 billion people who have ever lived on this planet, they would find just one ...

Why Jesus? Because nobody in human history has demonstrated in his life, death and resurrection that his claims to be God are true.

7 Why Jesus?

So far, we have looked at six answers to the question 'Why Jesus?' None is a rehashing of religious ideas; each of them is grounded in historical events that give them down to earth integrity.

His coming was announced in the Bible hundreds of years before he was born, and these prophecies included naming the exact place of his birth, stating that his mother would be a virgin when she gave birth to him, detailing some of the amazing miracles he would perform, giving details of his betrayal by one of his followers and forecasting in amazing detail his humiliating execution by a method not practised by his nation.

His virgin conception not only fulfilled prophecies made centuries earlier, but was documented by men whose professions demanded meticulously accuracy, and the miraculous birth that followed has no pagan parallel.

His life has never been equalled in word, action or character. His strongest enemies admitted, *No one ever spoke like this man* (John 7:46) and even when he claimed that he was the promised Messiah *all spoke well of him and marvelled at the gracious words that were coming from his mouth* (Luke 4:22). He performed countless astonishing miracles, including the healing of people with serious physical, mental, psychological and spiritual problems, and in unique contrast to the records of 'faith healers' past and present there is no recorded case of a false healing or a relapse. He even raised several people from the dead. Uniquely in human culture, he was without a moral, ethical or spiritual defect of any kind; he was absolutely perfect. When he asked his severest critics, *Which one of you convicts me of sin?* (John 8:46) there was silence—there still is ...

His own death was unique in two major ways. In the first place it was voluntary. Death is the inevitable outworking of *the law of sin and death* (Romans 8:2) but Jesus had no sin and was outside that law's jurisdiction. He died because he chose to do so. He told his followers, *No one takes* [my life] *from me, but I lay it down of my own accord* (John 10:18). He did not mean that he was about to commit suicide, but that he had complete authority over the whole process of dying. As some has said, 'He gave up his life because he willed it, when he willed it and as he willed it.' In the second place his death was on behalf of others and in their place, taking upon himself the penalty their sin deserved, then paying it in full —because he loved them.

His is the only complete resurrection in human history. As we have already seen, he raised other people from the dead (and God performed the same miracle a few times in Old Testament history) but all of those raised from the dead died again. Jesus never did: *We know that Christ being raised from the dead will never die again; death no longer has dominion over him. For the death he died he died to sin, once for all, but the life he lives he lives to God* (Romans 6:9-10). Because he took the sins of others upon himself, and became as accountable for them as if he had committed them, there was a point at which death did have dominion over him; he endured everything that it means and implies. But his resurrection shows that he paid in full the penalty laid down by *the law of sin and death*. He satisfied all of its demands, then overcame death itself by rising from the dead, having died to sin *once for all*. Because the death penalty had been paid in full, *it was not possible for him to be held by it* (Acts 2:24), so that he is now able to say, *I am the first and the last, and the living one. I died, and behold I am alive for evermore* (Revelation 1:17-18). C. S. Lewis put it perfectly: 'He has forced open a door that had been locked since the death of the first man. He has met, fought and beaten the King of Death. Everything is different because he has done so. This is the beginning of the new creation. A new chapter in cosmic history has opened.'

Finally, we saw the best possible answer to the question 'Why Jesus?', which is the mass of evidence proving not only his humanity but his divinity. There was a time when Jesus was God but not man, but ever since his birth there has never been a time when he was man but not God. He did not become a mixture of God and man. Instead, in coming from heaven to earth he took upon himself human nature, which he had never previously possessed. He added humanity to his divinity, and from then on has remained both God and man, with two natures in one personality. In the Bible's words, *In him the whole fullness of deity dwells bodily* (Colossians 2:9).

And so ....?

With all of the above in mind, you now face two inescapable questions. The first is perfectly straightforward and can be looked at very briefly, but it paves the way for the second, which you need to think through very carefully, as it calls for a life-changing response.

The first question is this: What do you think of Jesus? Countless people are prepared to say no more than that he was a good man and a great moral teacher, but that response makes no sense, because Jesus claimed to be God. If he was lying, then he was not a good man; if he was telling the truth, then merely calling him a good man will not do. C. S. Lewis is exactly right:

> Either this man was, and is, the Son of God; or else a madman or something worse. You can shut him up for a fool, you can spit at him and kill him as a demon, or you can fall at his feet and call him Lord and God. But let us not come up with any patronizing nonsense about his being a great moral teacher. He has not left that open to us. He did not intend to.

Jesus was either much more than a good man and a great moral teacher or he was neither. To say that he was right in most of his teaching but wrong in the most important claim he made about himself makes no sense. What do you think of him? He made it clear that coming to the right conclusion about his identity is hugely important by telling his critics, *Unless you believe that I am* [the eternal Son of God] *you will die in your sins* (John 8:24). You urgently need to settle this in your mind!

The second question is this: What will you do with him? At the end of this final chapter we will look at the options, but there is one particular thing that makes the question critically important: one day you will meet him. After Jesus rose from the dead and spent some time with his followers he *was taken up into heaven and sat down at the right hand of God* (Mark 16:19). But the time is coming when he will return to the earth, not this time as a helpless baby but as the judge of all mankind who will establish the kingdom of God on *a new heaven and a new earth* (Revelation 21:1).

The future return of Jesus to the earth is mentioned 300 times in the New Testament, never once as a theory or a possibility, but always as a certainty. We can therefore be sure it will happen, and that when it does *he will judge the world in righteousness* (Acts 17:31). We saw in Chapter 4 that death never means termination, and the Bible not only tells us that *it is appointed for man to die once' but adds 'and after that comes judgement* (Hebrews 9:27). Elsewhere it makes it clear that *each of us will give an account of himself to God* (Romans 14:12), who *has fixed a day on which he will judge the world in righteousness by a man whom he has appointed; and of this he has given assurance to all by raising him from the dead* (Acts 17:31). This is obviously Jesus, and confirms that the day is coming when you will stand before him and account for every moment of your life.

As he has already told us that *nothing is covered that will not be revealed, or hidden that will not be known* (Matthew 10:26) and as the Bible says elsewhere that *nothing unclean will ever enter* [heaven], *nor anyone who does what is detestable or false* (Revelation 21:27) how does your life match up to the demands of God's law? When asked which was the greatest of the commandments Jesus replied, *Love the Lord your God with all your heart and with all your soul and with all your mind and with all your strength* (Mark 12:30). This was a brilliant summary of the first four of the Ten Commandments, those which deal with our relationship to God. Jesus then followed it with an equally brilliant summary of the last six: *You shall love your neighbour as yourself* (Mark 12:31). These cover personal relationships, at home, at work, at school, college or university, in leisure hours and everywhere else. Looking back over your every thought, word and action during even the past week, is your conscience absolutely clear? Have you been perfectly kind, honest, humble, loving and pure at all times? Even if you are able to plead that you have avoided gross sins such as murder or adultery, you will have to reckon with Jesus' teaching that hatred is as sinful as murder and impure thinking the mental equivalent of adultery. You may be able to claim that you have never been guilty of child abuse, drug pushing, larceny or violent assault, what about other sins such as pride, envy, greed, selfishness, bitterness, anger, covetousness and jealousy? What about sins of the tongue, such as lying, slander, gossip, destructive criticism, unkindness and foul language? And what about those things you have failed to do? The Bible says, *Whoever knows the right thing to do and fails to do it, for him it is sin* (James 4:17). Have you always done all the good things you possibly could? Has every thought, word and action been such that not even God could find fault with it? The Bible asks, *Who can say, "I have made my heart pure; I am clean from my sin"?* (Proverbs 20:9). The question is personal and inescapable—and you know the answer. Although we may not all have sinned in the same way, or to the same extent, or with the same knowledge of what we were doing, one thing is certain—we have all sinned, and one sin is sufficient to make us lawbreakers in the sight of a pure and holy God and deserving of his judgement. Then think again about what Jesus called the greatest of all the Commandments. Have you truly loved God with all your heart, soul, mind and strength? If not, then surely you have committed (and are still committing) the greatest sin?

Anyone for heaven?

From what you have just read you may feel there is no hope for you (or for anyone else) but that would be a mistake. However, to assume that in spite of your sin God will sweep it all under the carpet and you will go to heaven is to make an equally serious mistake. Jesus said that comparatively few were on *the way ... that leads to life*, while many were on *the way ... that leads to destruction* (Matthew 7:13-14). It is urgently important for you to know whether you are one of the many or one of the few. Yet these are not two options from which God invites you to choose, because by nature you are already going the wrong way. As the Bible puts it, *All we like sheep have gone astray; we have turned every one to his own way* (Isaiah 53:6). What is needed is not a choice but a change, because if you stay as you are this present life is the best you will ever know and at the end of it you will face God's righteous judgement. If you refuse to recognize this, there is no hope for you.

But there is hope! Because of his love for us God came into the world in the person of his Son, Jesus Christ, to rescue sinners from sin's appalling penalty and to bring them into a living relationship with himself, both in this life and in the life to come. Jesus made his mission statement clear when he said that he *came to seek and to save the lost* (Luke 19:10). This is what the Bible calls the 'gospel', a word that means 'good news'—and it is the best news you will ever hear. If you were drowning at sea and unable to swim, it would be wonderful if somebody threw you a lifebelt—but you would not be saved unless you took hold of it. The writer of Hebrews warns his readers about the danger of ending up the same way as many Israelites did in the Old Testament. God had spoken to them, *but the message they heard did not benefit them, because they were not united by faith with those who listened* (Hebrews 4:2).

Jesus made it clear what response you need to make to receive the forgiveness of sins and eternal life. The very first recorded words he spoke in his public ministry were these: *The time is fulfilled, and the kingdom of God is at hand. Repent and believe in the gospel* (Mark 1:15). A few years later the apostle Paul called people to *repentance towards God and … faith in our Lord Jesus Christ* (Acts 20:21). The remaining pages of this book will spell out what the words 'repentance' and 'faith' mean. There are three things to say about each.

Repentance towards God is much more than regret or self-pity. Firstly, it means a change of mind about sin. It means realizing that sin— all sin—is not something that can be shrugged off as an excusable weakness, an error of judgement, or masked in some other way. Sin is not trivial, but terrible. It is not superficial, but something deep-rooted in the human heart. It is not a toy, but a killer. Sin separates us from God; if you truly repent you will change your mind about sin.

Secondly, repentance means a change of heart about sin. In a famous parable Jesus told, a rebellious son returned home and confessed to his father, *I have sinned against heaven and before you* (Luke 15:21). Genuine repentance will leave you deeply ashamed because you have broken God's holy law.

Thirdly, repentance means a change of will about sin. Israel's King David is a good example of this. He had sinned big-time, including adultery and being an accessory to murder, but when he came to his senses he pleaded with God, *Create in me a clean heart, O God, and renew a right spirit within me* (Psalm 51:10). He genuinely wanted to lead a new, clean life that was pleasing to God. Is this what you want? Self-centred sorrow is concerned only with what sin has done to you, or you may experience genuine remorse because you have hurt someone else, but God-centred sorrow grieves over the fact that your sin has offended God. He responds to true repentance with this life-changing promise: *Let the wicked forsake his way, and the unrighteous man his thoughts; let him return to the Lord, that he may have compassion on him, and to our God, for he will abundantly pardon* (Isaiah 55:7).

A few months after I had been interviewed on a BBC television program, a friend embarrassed me by repeating several things I had said in the studio before and after the interview. Unknown to me, every word had been recorded elsewhere in the building, and my friend had got hold of the tape. He hugely enjoyed replaying it at my expense, but it will be no laughing matter for you to stand before God, as one day you must, and be reminded of everything you have thought, said and done during your life on earth. Repentance is not a soft option, nor is it easily done. As someone has said, 'Like a well-worn pair of jeans, our [sinful] nature is easy to slip on and live in. Sin is what we know best as fallen creatures, and it is simple for us to go with what we know.' Yet refusing to turn from sin means *storing up wrath for yourself on the day of wrath when God's righteous judgement will be revealed* (Romans 2:5).

As with repentance, faith also involves the mind, the heart and the will. Firstly, it involves the mind: *Without faith it is impossible to please* [God], *for whoever would draw near to God must believe that he exists and that he rewards those who seek him* (Hebrews 11:6). This is faith at its most basic, as it is obviously not possible to get right with God if you do not believe that he even exists. But this faith includes believing the Bible's testimony about Jesus, which says that he is *the true God and eternal life* (1 John 5:20).

Secondly, true faith also involves the heart. In one of the Bible's best-known verses David wrote, *The Lord is **my** shepherd* (Psalm 23:1) (emphasis added), and the apostle Paul wrote of *the Son of God, who **loved me** and gave himself **for me*** (Galatians 2:20) (emphasis added). Writing to early New Testament Christians about Jesus, the apostle Peter told them, *Though you have not seen him, you love him* (1 Peter 1:8). Peter had spent a lot of time with Jesus, and had met with him after his resurrection. On almost the last time they met, Jesus asked him whether he loved him, and Peter replied, *Lord, you know everything; you know that I love you* (John 21:17). Peter had been one of his inner circle of friends. He had seen him in private and in public, and had ample opportunity to hear what he said and see what he did. As a result, he had not only come to believe Jesus was *the Christ, the Son of the living God* (Matthew 16:16), he had come to know and love him as a personal friend. True faith will draw you to do the same.

Thirdly, faith in Jesus goes even further; it involves the will. It means not only trusting him to save you from the punishment your sin deserves but committing yourself to him as your Lord. If you were planning to fly somewhere it would not be enough to have detailed and accurate information about the airline, or even to believe that the pilot was capable of flying you to your destination. You would need to trust him and commit yourself to him by boarding the aircraft. In the same way, turning to Jesus Christ in faith means no longer trusting in your own moral or spiritual efforts, but 'getting on board' by trusting him and him alone to save you from the guilt and consequences of your sin.

Some years ago I was in Jerusalem and needed to find a post office. As I was completely lost, I asked a shopkeeper to help me. He began by giving me a long list of instructions (the oldest part of the city is a maze of streets and alleyways) but when he noticed that I was getting confused he glanced at the time, pulled down the shutters of his tiny shop and said, 'Come with me, I am the way.' I stuck to him like glue and was soon where I wanted to be. Jesus said, *I am the way, and the truth, and the life. No one comes to the Father except through me* (John 14:6). I urge you to turn to him now, to confess your sin, to cast yourself upon him as the only one who can save you, and to commit yourself to your Creator, who loves you and has a prior claim on your life.

Why Jesus? Because you will meet him one day, either as your Judge or as your Saviour.

Those who meet him as Judge will spend eternity exposed for ever to God's righteous anger, punishment infinitely greater than we have ever experienced or could ever imagine.

Those who meet him as Saviour will spend eternity in his holy presence, where they will know *an eternal weight of glory beyond all comparison* (2 Corinthians 4:17) and experience *fullness of joy* and *pleasures for evermore* (Psalm 16:11).

Why not you?